ANTHOLOGY OF POETRY
BY
YOUNG AMERICANS®

2002 EDITION
VOLUME CLXXIII

Published by Anthology of Poetry, Inc.

©*Anthology of Poetry by Young Americans*®
2002 Edition
Volume CLXXIII
All Rights Reserved©

Printed in the United States of America

To submit poems
for consideration in the year 2003 edition of the
Anthology of Poetry by Young Americans®,
send to: poetry@asheboro.com or

> Anthology of Poetry, Inc.
> PO Box 698
> Asheboro, NC 27204-0698

Authors responsible
for originality of poems submitted.

The Anthology of Poetry, Inc.
307 East Salisbury • P.O. Box 698
Asheboro, NC   27204-0698

Paperback ISBN: 1-883931-33-9
Hardback ISBN: 1-883931-32-0

Anthology of Poetry by Young Americans®
is a registered trademark of
Anthology of Poetry, Inc.

Our scattered flocks at play in the fields on that crystal-blue morning.

It has been a year where we've seen our rivers of faith run momentarily backward, heard our symphonic voice of unity splinter into a cacophony of cries, and felt our hearts pull tight with the erratic beat of panic. It has been the year when we found our collective soul, and reconstituted our American fiber.

In the thirteen years since the first Anthology of Poetry by Young Americans® was published, no single school year has meant so much to the parents, children, and dedicated teachers. This has been a year where we've seen the hearts of our young fill with hope and worry, uncertainty and faith, with love and anger. In the eyes of our children we've seen the look of need, the expression of love, and the want of new words. As time stood still and the force of survival demanded their strength, they grew before our very eyes. We held them close and we wiped their tears. To us, they gave back hope.

Let us now listen. It is time for the youth of this great country to share with us their thoughts, to share with us their vision, to share with us their promise of an American future.

Gather now our scattered flocks at play in the fields on this crystal-blue morning…

Our growing family at the Anthology of Poetry, Inc. sends our love, sympathies, and hope to the thousands of families forever changed on the morning of September 11, 2001.

The Editors

THE BISON

"Once upon a time,"
I told my son,
"On the prairie, roamed
Thousands of bison.

A resource for many to use
Every part of the animal's inside,
A teepee was built
From the buffalo's hide.

The meat was good to eat,
The fat was used for frying.
Horns made combs, that removed
Tangles without crying!

The bones for tools,
The sinew for lace.
Soon came the white men
Destroying herds at an incredible pace."

Colten Rohleder
Age: 8

THE PARTY

The Party
She went to the party but never came home.
The Party
The music was loud and she felt so alone.
The Party
He asked her to dance and he swept her away.
The Party
She was finally happy
But her life changed that day.
The Party
They came over and told her
She was part of the clique.
The Party
She had tasted peer pressure
And she liked what she licked.
The Party
They pressured her on and finally she did.
The Party
They passed her a bottle
And she popped off the lid.
The Party
She jumped in the car her goal had been reached.
The Party
She slammed on the brakes
And heard was a screech.

The Party
Some choices she made cost her life and her fame.
The Party
Her family will always remember her name.
The Party
They got over her death
But she was never forgotten.
The Party
Their lives changed forever all because of
The Party.

Jaclyn Nichole Leonard
Age: 11

Spider soup, goblin, gummies,
Mage, magic, witch, worms,
Skeleton, sky, vampire, vermits,
Mummy walks the night.

Kirsten Staples
Age: 8

Molly
nice, loving
sleeping, barking, growling
my cute dog
Golden retriever

Lauren Green
Age: 8

Grape
fruity, nutritious
rolling, smelling, sharing
oh so fruity
Fruit

Andrew Phillips
Age: 8

COPPER

Copper
fantastic, protective
barking, growling, snarling
ramming into walls
Puppy

Ally Fanning
Age: 8

SUMMER RAIN

Pit, Pat on my umbrella.
Split, Splat on my hand.
Lean back the taste is sweet and cold.
The cool rain washes away the heat
On this scorching summer day.
Bare feet slip on soggy grass,
My toes wiggle and grass sticks to them.
I fold my umbrella
And let cool wetness envelop me.
A drop rolls off my nose onto my tongue.
I skip, I hop, my feet squelching
In the grass and mud.
I'm completely soaked, but oh,
Glory be to rain!

Maura Williams
Age: 11

B eautiful
R ight-handed
I ncredible
T errific
T iny
A mazing
N ice
Y oung

Brittany Verbeke
Age: 8

Popcorn
salty, buttery
crunching, pulling, eating
The taste of popcorn is delightful.
Food

Eric Verbeke
Age: 8

If I were a Beaufort Seven
I'd carry birds swiftly through the air
On my shoulders.
The trees would sway
Like dancers bowing to an audience.
I'd make the animals bark and meow with alarm.
I'd smell like soil that had been freshly dug.
I'd dribble rain
Like little balls bouncing on the hardwood floor.
Leaves would begin to circle into the air
And dash away.
I would feel so delighted when people scoot inside
As I whip by their houses at 32-38 m.p.h.
I would sound like water splashing on windows
As I passed the last house on the block.
People would have trouble
Walking against my stiff breath.
Shingles would propel from roofs
And flags would rise to hail the morning
As the ocean waves turn white.
I'd feel strong and powerful.

Genell Britton
Age: 8

RAINBOWS

Bright against the sky
A mystic arch of beauty
Bold colorful streams

Nicole Kay Lewton
Age: 11

SEPTEMBER 11TH

People screaming
I'm not there
but I can still hear the screams
I say
why did they do this?
Oh why oh why?
They made me cry and cry
they shattered innocent lives
and made us cry
in that burning wreckage
why did they
do that to
our hearts
our lives
our dreams

Kelsey Murray
Age: 11

Hurricane
destructive, reckless
killing, twirling, flying
monster, storm, breeze, happiness
flowing, playing, dancing,
gentle, cool
Calm

Richard Barz
Age: 8

WHEN MY DOG WENT AWAY

It was a beautiful day,
But when my dog went away,
My day was sad, and the week was bad.
I had my dog for a long time,
Until he ate a sour lime.
He ran away with a puckered face,
Then came back to his normal place.

Lindsay Packard
Age: 9

SPARKLING WATER

Shimmering and sparkling as the
blazing sun just begins to rise...
And the moon slowly dies.
Feeling cool and soothing against my skin.
Swirling wildly with the strong, strong wind.
Oh so clear, as clear as glass.
Rushing swiftly in a very large mass.
Dripping down my back.
Chills running through my spine.
I wish all the water could just be mine.
Gently lapping at the sandy shore.
Calmed completely when the sun is no more.

Melody Ypsilantis

A WORLD

I live in a world
Where God's law no longer exists.
I live in a world
Where people don't care about anything --
Anything -- but themselves

I live in a world
Of murder and adultery.
I live in a world
Of hunger, pain, and longing --
Hunger and longing for God's word

I live in a world
Where people are blind.
I live in a world
Which is blinded by its own pride
Enough not to see others' needs
As well as their own

I live in a world
Of hate and war.
I live in a world
Where hurt brings joy --
Empty and meaningless joy

I live in a world
That is filthy, like rags.
I live in a world
With a deep hidden need --
A need they can't give to themselves.

But there is a world
With a law built with love.
But there is a world
Where people do care --
They care -- about other people

But there is a world
Of love and truth.
But there is a world
Of plenty, joy, and fulfillment --
For those who know Him

But there is a world
Where eyes are opened.
But there is a world
Which is vigilant by faith --
Faith -- that they have in their God

But there is a world
With peace and happiness.
But there is a world
Where hope brings joy --
A deep and fulfilling joy

But there is a world
With perfect harmony
But there is a world
With every need met --
By the One who is greater than all.

So now I'm asking you
To join a world that knows no sin
Now I'm asking you
To be in the world --
In it, but not of it

Alyssa Nichole Davidson
Age: 14

THE AMERICAN SOULS

We're strong and brave,
We gave our lives
To our fellow Americans,
We cherish, we love, we care.

We save lives,
We gave lives,
We lived lives.

United we stand.

Parker Smith
Age: 8

MY CAT LILLY

I have a cat named "Lilly,"
She is very silly!
She likes to eat fish,
Just like her best friend "Milly."
They went to the park,
Where it was very chilly!
So skipping on home,
They're back to playing silly.
I love her so!!!

Katelyn Gray
Age: 8

AMERICA

Bright lights shining through neighborhoods.
Flags, soaring over driveways.
Doctors healing fragile humans.
Firefighters fighting for lives.
People caring for evey soul they see.
Armies fighting for freedom.
Loving, caring, intelligent people helping others.
Warm-hearted donating blood and money.
When horrible people do horrible things
Like the Twin Towers.

Samuel W. Kilman
Age: 11

SOCCER!

Soccer is fun.
Kicking.
Running.
Making scores.
Soccer is really cool!

Alex Truitt
Age: 7

PUPPERONI

Pupperoni is my puppy.
She is cute.
She is fun.
She can run.
She jumps.
I love my puppy!

Rachel Hawkins
Age: 7

WINNING

The boat enters the harbor
  I turn him.
Heads turn toward the statue
  10 to 0 -- screaming fills the gym.
Pride makes me the best
  pride fills you with energy
Torch held high
  arm raised
like the Statue of Liberty
  I represent happiness.
People stare in satisfaction
I made it
  I won!

Kory Love
Age: 12

DOGS

I have a dog,
Her name is Molly.
She is cute, I wish you could see her.
She has floppy ears, she is fat,
She chases deer and sometimes a rat.
She has toys that make sounds,
When she hears them, off she bounds!

Rachel Stichler
Age: 8

THE DRIVE

A loose grip on the wheel,
Like the loose grip on her life,
Drives the Chevy onward.

Bad 80's music blares in the background
And unwary street signs flash
Like angry memories.

An endless ribbon of tainted asphalt,
Painfully straight,
Accompany the sterile rows
Of telephone wire and corn.

This is the night it rained tears.

Cali Pfaff
Age: 15

EXCLAMATION POINT

I'm always happy
I'm never sad
People use me to indicate glad
I'm rarely seen when mad
Because I'm the exclamation
Point!
!

Brennan Lammermann
Age: 11

EMOTIONS

My emotions are a river,
flowing fast and hard,
then calming like a spring rain,
soothing to my heart.
Sometimes my emotions fill me up,
then leave me cold and dry;
sometimes I feel like bursting out,
sometimes I want to cry.
I float around high in the air
on a cloud of pure bliss;
then I fall back to the ground,
those good feelings I do miss.
'Round and 'round my emotions spin,
like an endless top;
though they rarely keep a pace,
they will never stop.

Roxanne T. Abell
Age: 13

SKY

Beneath the blue sky flowers shine bright.
The clouds look down at the world.
When it's beautiful, they smiley pretty.
I look at the sky -- it's pretty.

Reyna Vigil
Age: 7

BROWN

Brown is the color of my favorite teddy bear
He looks so sad just sitting there.
Brown is the color of my daddy's new shirt
It's also his frown when he's feeling hurt.

Brown is the color of a little bird's nest
It's also the color of a big bear's chest.
Brown is the ground all covered with dirt
Brown is the color of toast when it's burnt.

Brown is the sound of a baby's soft cry
He whimpers for his mother
When she's not nearby.
Brown is the color of a chestnut mare
It's also the color of my long straight hair.

Juliana Millbern - Bell
Age: 10

I am a toolmaker
I made the tools out of rocks
I make the corners razor-sharp
I use the tools to crack open bones
I work until dark

Emily M. Cho

AMERICA IS BEAUTIFUL

America is green grass growing,
America is sand,
America is beautiful.

America is great big trees,
America is shining seas,
America is beautiful.

America is fifty states,
America is three great oceans,
America is beautiful.

America is mountaintops,
America is grassy fields,
America is beautiful.

America is everything
You could make up in your mind,
America is beautiful.

Brandon Fenner
Age: 9

THE ONION

Bitter and papery,
The skin flakes off in my
Hand.
The translucent flesh almost,
But not quite lets me see the
Inside core.
Slicing the layers lets off a
Sharp scent.
Enough to make me cry,
The salty tears make
Tracks down my cheeks
And the rivers will not be dammed.
If I wait long enough,
Maybe she will let me peel away
The outside and find what
She's hiding.
Maybe.
The cooked flesh is sweet on
My tongue,
Delicious, perfect and slippery.
I pinch the shell too hard.
She is gone. Slipped between
My fingers, down the drain,
Never to be seen again.
My sister is the onion.

Melissa Murray
Age: 14

GOD BLESS THE U. S. A.

When you thought we weren't looking
We saw you rescue a kitten from a tree
And we knew you cared

When you thought we weren't looking
We saw you stop a fire
And we knew how much you loved your job

When you thought we weren't looking
We saw you save a life
And we learned to care

When you thought we weren't looking
We saw New York
And we cried for all of you

When you though we weren't looking
We looked
And saw all the things that make you heroes

Chelsea Krause
Age: 9

WINTER

When I smell winter I smell hot cocoa
letting off a wonderful fragrance.

When I hear winter, I hear the wind
howling like a coyote.

When I feel winter, I feel icy snowflakes
melting on my warm tongue.

When I see winter, I see children having snowball fights
with bullet-moving snowballs.

When I taste winter I taste freshly-made
Santa-shaped cookies warming up my body
with their gooey flavor.

Using my senses, I smell, hear, feel, see
and taste winter with all its wonderful sensations.

Alexis Fowler
Age: 10

I am Lucy
I eat berries
I live in a tree
I don't eat meat
I eat bugs

Sarah Magid

MY MOTHER

M y mom is very nice.
Y o Mom!

M y mom washes my clothes.
 O utstanding my mother is
 T he best!
s H e is the best!
 E very day my clothes are clean
 R arely they are dirty.
     She always takes me everywhere
     And I love it!

Ben Larson

MY DOG

I like my dog.
My dog is the best.
He runs.
He jumps.
He lays.
He plays.
He is cool.
I love my dog!

Dymond Braun
Age: 8

MY FRIEND

Will is...
silly
intelligent
the most fun I've ever had
cool
nice as can be
good at sports
great at video games
the best friend anyone could ever have
makes you feel good when you feel bad

Chase Turri

AMERICA

I am proud to live in America.
To live in her many cities and watch the sunrise.
To look at her high mountain peaks and gaze at the sky.
To see her many oceans and watch the waves go by.
To see her many states.
To sit on her riverbanks
   and see all the plants and animals.
To eat her many foods and drink her many drinks.
To watch her sunset over rolling hills.
I am proud to live in America.

Alexander Lazear
Age: 9

BUTTERFLIES

Red, green, and blue
As they travel through the fields,
All saying look at me!

Lindsey Butler
Age: 12

SHINING THROUGH

Firefighters, courage,
Police officers, bravery
Putting their lives
On the line for us,
They are always
a shining star,
Firefighters walk out
Of a fire with a baby in their arms
Makes us cry,
They come shining through.
Police officers
Hunting down criminals,
Police officers involved in a shootout
Then walk out alive,
This police officer is shining through.
We love to see them
Shining through.

Mae Fischbach

COLORS

The bright yellow sun
Rises through the window.
The brown rooster crows.
The black cow goes moo!
The white snow
Floats down.
The pink pig goes "oink."
The blue sky is light.
There goes the orange
School bus.
Life is full of
Colors.

Shelby Cunningham
Age: 11

COURAGE

C ourage
O utstanding
yo U are the best
R unning
A lways there
G reat
E verything to me

Jonathan McVay

HALLOWEEN

Halloween, Halloween,
a favorite day from tots to teens.
Girls are often princesses,
dancing around in their pretty dresses.
You'll see boys as superheroes,
eating their candy down to zeros.
Then there are those in-between,
the ghosts and goblins that make adults scream.
The only time you'll see things so keen,
is on Halloween, Halloween.

Katie Weingardt

HAROLD COME

My owners calling out a name
For whom I don't know
She is staring right at me
She is saying "move go"
I'm not ignoring you
I just can't remember my name

Erin McMahon

PENCILS

Pencils are great even though pencils can break
Pencils can erase
Pencils can write "Boo" to you
Pencils can travel to Hawaii or New York
Or even to Europe
Pencils can get dirty
Pencils are great.

Kelly Lynch
Age: 7

THANK YOU

Thank you for my sense of sight.
    It helps me see the darkest of night.
Thank you for my sense of smell.
    It helps me enjoy life very well.
Thank you for my sense of touch.
    It helps me catch balls very much.
Thank you for my sense of taste.
    It always brings joy to my face.
Thank you for my sense of sound.
    It helps me enjoy myself all around.

Sam Holz
Age: 10

THE BLUE OCEAN

I am a beautiful little fairy princess
In a lemonade swimming pool
With an astonishing noggin
Who would like to be floating
In the pretty blue ocean

Nathan Bellowe
Age: 6

Fingernails are vulgar pieces of God's art,
filled with crusty layers of dry crumbly filth.
Plowing underneath the outer shell,
a shovel scoops out the deposit of a week's work.

Stabbing away with an unnoticed blade,
causing red rivers and painful open pits.
They will catch on linens,
unraveling them until there is nothing left.

Some make them pretty,
with paints and others alike.
Fingernails aren't buildings,
why not leave them hideous and atrocious?

Like pieces of grass they keep growing on,
until you chop them off with a snap.
Weeks of labor, pain and sweat,
is flicked away by yet another fingernail.

Morgan Evans
Age: 14

GENERATION UPON GENERATION

Through the sea
  We come to be,
All filthy and slimy as can be.
  Now we're all a scaly creature,
Roaming the land,
  Always in danger.
Climbing trees is what we do,
  Always in fear and on the move.
Building fires to cook our prey,
  And sculpting out of sticky clay.
On the seas we sail about,
  Looking for land while creating a route.
Often we gather to talk of our plans,
  To start a settlement and our own clans.
Through the dusty streets we travel,
  By horseback and carts.
We sew with yarn that unravels,
  And we help the sailors by making charts.
Now we pack up and leave for the West,
  Traveling by wagon with some old chest.
We struggle to survive,
  Though we know we will always thrive
  In the wilderness.
Immigrants travel and arrive by ship,
  Though we might trip,
While in the line to truly be in Freedom Land.
  Finally, a new time comes.

Cars go by, children run.
   New fashions are so strange,
Though now the earth is arranged,
   In certain ways
That always shows,
   That the world is a different place.

Katherine M. Daniel
Age: 10

LEGO'S

Lego's are cool!
Lego's are fun!!
I wish we had them at school,
   For I like them a ton!!!
Maybe I could use them to make a pool,
   Or maybe a hamburger bun?!
Lego's rule...
Maybe I could make the sun!?!

Aaron Fisher Gould
Age: 8

DRY MY TEARS

Dry my tears when I cry
Offer me your shoulder when I feel down
Dry my tears when I feel sad
Make my heart feel lighter when I am mad
Dry my tears when I feel sorrow
Try to understand when I hurt inside
Dry my tears when I get into a fight
Help me when it looks like I need it
Dry my tears when we get into a fight
Give your hand when I feel scared
Dry my tears when I am crying
Because I am happy
Give me a hug or kiss
When it looks like I need it
Dry my tears when you see me cry
Give me inspiration
When you think I need an idea
Dry my tears and hold me close.

Laura Carey
Age: 14

BUTTERFLIES

I'm playing outside
Lots of butterflies fly by
Bye-bye butterflies

Avery Meersman
Age: 9

FALL

Crispy, crunchy, rusty leaves
Float whiskily to the ground.
Dancing, prancing in the wind.
At night the small fireflies come out
On and off, on and off, on and off fluttering about
Seeking every little cold light.

Madeline O'Connell
Age: 8

HOW DO YOU EXPLAIN?
A poem of the Holocaust

How do you explain to a child
When he cries, that his mother is gone
She'll never kiss or hug him again
To the Nazi's, she's just a pawn.

How do you explain to a child
What's happened to his grandpa, too
He went to the left, you know
As all the old ones do.

How do you explain to a child
The piles and piles of clothes on the ground
Along with the hair and the many shoes
Which will never be reclaimed or found.

How do you explain to a child
The stench of burning that fills the air
You can't tell him that it's death
Of people forced into the hungry lion's lair.

How do you explain to a child
What goes on inside the "showers"
How, when one walks in,
One knows it's the devil's bower.

How do you explain to a child
Why his life has gone all wrong
He may never sing or dance or play
His life could end with this sad song.

How do you explain to a child
Why his friends have gone away
When he is fortunate enough
To have stood the test of days.

How do you explain to a child
Why his relatives and friends are all gone
When this terrible trial is over
Why he's the only one?

Brynn Lewallen
Age: 16

If I were a light breeze
I'd calmly brush your gazing eyes.
Flags would ripple and rise
like rolling ocean waves.
Chimney smoke would gracefully glide,
and wind vanes would stand tall
watching the early morning sunrise.
Birds would soar through my extended arms
and would fly lightly
through the yellow light of day.
I would wake kids from their beds
as adults call them to the table for breakfast.
I'd sway tree limbs
and make you put on a light overcoat.
I'd guide clusters of laughing children
off to school and life would be fine.

Kylie Youmans
Age: 9

BEIGE

Beige is the color of a beach's sand
Beige is the color of a fire-burned land.
When the color beige comes to mind
I think of sandpaper, rough and not lined,

Beige is the color of smog in the city
Beige can be the color of a newborn kitty,
Beige is the sound of wind in bare trees
Beige can be the sound of someone's pleas,

Beige is also sad when you feel
You don't belong, you don't appeal,
Beige is fall, beige is winter
And beige is when you get a splinter,

Beige is neat and is a light brown
Beige is the color of dust in a town.
Beige is the tail of a cute little opossum
Beige is so cool, it's totally awesome!

Victoria E. Kelly
Age: 10

SHE IS LIFE

She is life and life is she.
She is one who lets us swim in her sea.
She is the reason that life is here.
She gives us water, not dirty but clear.
The flowers, the mountains, she made it all.
You can thank her,
but don't expect someone to answer your call.
But when you hear the leaves
rustling in the wind, you'll know it's her.
She's saying you're welcome.
She's watching.
Watching not only you
but all the animals and plants.
Her creations.
So when you see a flower,
a rose or a posey.
Or three little four-year-olds
playing ring-around-the-rosy.
Or maybe a garden,
filled with peppers.
Maybe six playful newborn German shepherds.
Just know this,
she's smiling down on all of them.
Watching them grow.
Watching how her creations turned out.
Who is she you ask?
Why she is my mother,
· Mother Earth.

Stephanie Muller
Age: 10

As I sit here thinking
Under a roof of safety
With this paper and pen
To put my thoughts down on

A warm blanket under my feet
To keep me cozy all through the night

And a little furry friend at my side
Snoozing away the night.
You and me both know
The world is safe for now
Because of the citizens of America,
Our flag will fly with the wind.

Sean Bevins
Age: 9

FIRE AND ICE

Fire melts ice.
Ice freezes fire.
Fire is hot.
Ice is cold.
Fire burns.
Ice stings.
Fire and ice make cold light.
Ice and fire make hot light.

Thomas Rubio
Age: 14

On September 11th a sad event happened.
There were four planes hijacked and crashed
Into the Twin Towers, Pentagon,
A field in Pennsylvania and Washington.
The Twin Towers fell like falling blocks.
There was a big fire.
The planes that crashed in Pennsylvania
Fell in a field.
Many people died by fire,
The clasps of the building,
Or jumping out the windows.
Now we are bombing Afghanistan
To find bin Laden.
He was the one who planned the crashing.
Now innocent people are dying in Afghanistan.
Just so we can find bin Laden.
Bush gave them two chances to give him up
But they refused.
Now we still need to find him.
The whole world is on our side
Against terrorist attacks.

Matthew L. Bouley
Age: 11

TRAGEDY!

Flash!
A plane hit one of the Twin Towers
Confusion spread,
All around the nation
Televisions and radios turned on,
Waiting for what is going to happen next why?
Could it have been a simple mistake
Or was it on purpose,
Thinking a simple mistake had occurred,
People went back to their normal lives,
Thirty minutes later Boom! Flash!
There was silence,
More confusion spread,
The people of New York
And the nation were speechless,
What really happened nobody knows,
Lives of innocent people were taken
Just to prove somebody's point.
Later another flash struck for the people
Of New York only to gaze at
As the Pentagon turned into a triangle,
The people of Afghanistan rejoiced
as the south tower collapsed,
The President gave a speech,
The speech didn't really help the people
Who were paralyzed,
Firefighters, police officers, and paramedics
Rushed to the tragedy.
People donated blood
But they couldn't change the past.

Weeks later the United States
Struck and bombed Afghanistan,
Even though the terrorists didn't kill us,
They killed our souls --
So we need to stand united.

Mitchell Ottoson
Age: 10

WORLD!

W onderful life
O n this great planet
R eside the people and animals who
L ive here in peace and harmony
D edicated to making the world a better place
   World!

Allison Meyer
Age: 9

Paint your eyes like Cleopatra
Eyes like Egypt
Like the Nile
   Drinking in
      the sounds of water
         the sounds of birds
            the sounds of life,
pulsating and true.

Her eyes are drunk

That clear hard
green
   green and cool
      a room after sunset

In a land before camels
   before the turn of the hourglass

After the Nile has raged.

Cleopatra
      the north wind
half-goddess
      the other half beauty
   the cave of storm in the ships
of the wind
      The North Wind

Toy boats --
   the children -- tossed by the waves

Dark and white and blurry pink
In sea chests of iron and rotting wood
Waste away while she weeps her fate

On the cave floor
Strewn with rushes and grass

And the nest of black snakes
on coffee cream silk

Maryn Lewallen
Age: 14

THE BRIGHT LIGHT

The bright light in the sky
so very, very high.
Looks like a big ball -- a sun.
That bright light in the sky
shows God's love for everyone.

Justin Cox
Age: 8

MYSTERIOUS

He stands alone,
No friends to support,
No enemies to hate him.

He has never known fear,
He has never known anger,
He has never known love.

He's known beauty,
He knows nature,
He can read minds.

His life seems empty,
Yet it is full with life
That we will never know.

For we don't stand alone
We have friends to support us,
We have enemies that hate us.

We have known fear,
We have known anger,
We have known love.

We think we know beauty,
We think we know nature,
We can't read minds.

To him our life seems empty,
Yet it is full of life
That he will never know.

Does he envy us?
Do we envy him?
Will we ever know?

Sara Lauren Paliga
Age: 13

The crash aroused my flaming anger
It triggered sadness as deep as the sea
Immense sorrow pulses through my mind
My sympathy flows like a river
Baffling chaos spins me
Shocking fright spreads quick as lightning
Towering rage overcomes me
The Twin Towers explode in my mind
Yet we still stand strong
America's pride lives on
And deep in the hearts of the old and the young
Those Towers still stand up tall
We still follow our paths wherever they lead
On to greater things and better times
We track down our enemies
Our journey is not over
And we must not lose hope
For America thrives
More than our enemies could ever expect
We still have Twin Towers deep in our hearts
Standing tall and proud

Steven Medberry
Age: 10

A PERFECT DAY

The perfect day happens when all is good,
And beautiful birds are flying
In the bright blue sky.
The green grass is waving in the wind,
And flowers are blooming
Into many brilliant colors.

The perfect day is when the ocean's waves
Are rocking as gently as a baby cradle.
Life is happening and people are growing.
In the streets there is no traffic
And the lights stay green.

The perfect day is when the brook is
Winding its way through the land
Like a snake in the grass, and the trees are
Waving to you, saying hello and good-bye
As you walk past them.

The perfect day has a morning landscape
That is all green. The sunset is orange
And yellow and pink. Endless laughter
Fills the air. People will be jolly,
And full of joy. Nothing will go wrong
On this perfect day.

Ashton Coleman
Age: 13

THE GUARDIAN ANGEL

I can't believe it happened,
She is such a neat and caring woman.
When I held her hand,
She began to cry.
As the nurse began drilling the needle
Deep into her skin,
I began to cry.
The next day I bought her something...
It was a "Guardian Angel" pin.
As she lay there I began to gain hope,
Somewhere deep within I knew
That my grandma would live.
And she did...
Thank you guardian angel!!!

Tenae Allison
Age: 13

WHAT IS WONDERFUL?

Is it the soft, thin grass tickling my legs
Or is it the smell of nature
Because of the fresh fallen leaves
Or is it the sound of the breeze blowing over
The trees making leaves rattle
As a plane bellows above in the light, blue sky
As a huge cloud like an arrow aims towards me
Now what is not wonderful about that?

Christopher James Conway
Age: 10

STANDING TALL, BENEATH IT ALL

9/11 was a tragic day,
They came at us in a very frightening way

This attack affected us all,
It also caused many known structures to fall

We are going to come back strong
And we will fight,
Through the day and through the night

Hopefully we will take them down,
'Cause I know that's what we want in my town.

Ardell Halston
Age: 11

RAINBOWS

A rainbow is colorful
A rainbow is fun
A rainbow gives smiles to everyone
A rainbow is orange, red, blue,
Yellow, purple, and green.

A rainbow is very beautiful to see
A rainbow is fun
A rainbow gives smiles to everyone.

Abigail Sheldon
Age: 7

THANK YOU

You are always here for me in good times and bad,
You are the one who pulled me through.
You are the one who always stands by me
And helps me through,
You are the one who lifts me up
When I can't reach,
You pick me up when I fall down.
Even when everyone else has left me
You are still there by my side
Every step of the way
To comfort me, to hold me, to reassure me,
And just to be there
When I need somebody to talk to.
I would give the world for you,
When I am in a pinch you always pull me through.
When I am hurt or sad you always find some way
To make me feel better.
When others kick me down and leave me
You are still there for me.
When I need a shoulder to cry on
It is you I always go to,
I just want to say thank you
For everything you have ever done.
I am forever in your debt,
Thank you for always being here for me
And I want you to know
I will always be here for you.

Dedicated to all of my friends, family and teachers
Who have ever helped and or believed in me.

Leslie Koehn
Age: 13

BUBBLES

Bubbles are things all of us have
rich or poor black or white young and old
they are the hopes, dreams and wishes
of children, adults, and teenagers around the world
some bubbles will float high with the wind
like ships out on the sea or shooting stars
and comets in velvet blue sky
with all the universe and planets, stars,
and moons orbiting around the one
that brings us light and warmth
the sun shining brightly bringing the message
around the world "You are not alone"

Aubri Tharp
Age: 11

THE FLAME

The flame so bright flickering in the night
The only light burning about so rapidly
In the dark room
Lighting up the ghostly walls
Making shadows among them
The eyes of the flame the brightest part
Melting the candle wax
Outside it is getting light
I blow, the candle flickers
Glowing on the walls
I blow again, it's going, going, gone

Kaitlin LaFlamme
Age: 10

THANKSGIVING

T hrilling and you're
H appy and
A bout
N ice
K ind things
S taying with family
G iving thanks and sharing
I deas with family
V isiting and eating
I ce-cold drinks, being
N ear family
G iving love to each other.
  Thanksgiving!

Olivia Anderson
Age: 9

TOGETHER

T hanksgiving is
O n a special day
G etting together
E very year
T o
H ave a feast
E at and eat
R eally good turkey!
  Together!

Jessica Acheson
Age: 9

YELLOW

"Why is it," said the little bird
"That yellow smells so good?"
"I wouldn't know" said the wise old owl,
"Does it smell of wood?"
"Of course it could, it's anything you like,
For me I think of butter, or of daisies
Or of simply, well, delight!"
"Could you think of sunshine,
Or the opening of well-read books?"
"Of course you could," said the little bird,
"But what about its looks?"
"For looks," said the wise old bird,
Now very deep in thought,
"I think of bumblebees,
And the opposite of drought..."
"For me" dreamed the little bird,
Now quite off in space,
"I think of summer, or blankets,
Or golden bridges like gates."
"...The unwashed face of the moon,
Or a crunchy, bursting cocoon.
What of yellow's sound?"
The little bird said "To be heard!"
The owl said "you silly nerd!...

Yellow is the sound of summer,
Bursting at the seams,
Yellow is the sound of 'curious,'
And a thousand come true dreams."
"Good thoughts." Piped the little bird,
Not wanting to be forgot...
"In comparison,
What chance have other colors got?"

Kelli E. Brazier
Age: 14

FRIENDS

I have a whole bunch
of friends
yes I do
and they're all
really cool too
We have slumber parties
and popcorn too
with pop and secrets
to tell you
so you know you
can have friends too
so cool and neat too

Brenna Fujimoto
Age: 10

THE CASE OF THE MISSING DIAMOND

All dressed in blue
A detective ready to find a clue.
He decided to look for some evidence
In a lady's residence.
He sat at a phone booth
To try to figure out the truth.
He made a reservation
To finish his investigation.
He went on a cruise
Bumped his head and got a big bruise.
Oh look the diamond just in time
For the detective to solve the crime.

Nicklas Glass Decherd
Age: 10

BLACK

Venom spreading cold,
shuddering in the cold frost,
a dreamless sleep
falling through the chaos of smoke.
The shade of charred wood,
and a skyline at dusk,
the silhouette of an entertainer
beneath the fading stage lights.

Mike Houlihan
Age: 14

WINTER

Winter is pretty cold
but if you are by the fire it's warm
after each and every snowstorm
you could build a snowman
when all the snow melts
it seems as everyone yells
for all the fun
is all done

Connor Heaton
Age: 9

THANKSGIVING

T hanksgiving is a time to get together
H aving fun
A feast for a king is what I have on Thanksgiving
N ame-calling is prohibited
K nowing that people have pies
S aying grace over a turkey
G iving instead of getting
I n a room with candles
V ery plump and most delightful pies
encour I ng people for their most beliefs
N ana giving you more turkey
G et happy! It's Thanksgiving!

Amy Lee Howard
Age: 9

DIFFERENT PEOPLE GETTING WHAT THEY WANT

An illegitimate businessman, with a furtive glance
As cash bribes are stuffed in pockets
The hardworking student,
Slaving day and night over the books
The strong arm, with a warning meant to instill fear
An honest man, working tirelessly
With his ethics intact
The robber, and his implied threat
Of a revealed weapon
The wannabe starlet, willing to go to any length
To get a job
Another student, who gets his papers
Off the Internet
The lucky man, to whom good fortune
Seems to always come
The manipulator, using everything and everyone
To achieve his own ends
All trying to get what they want
Which way is most successful?
I guess we'll never know
But somehow, someway
They all get there

Laurenn Berger ·
Age: 14

HORSE

Your beautiful coat is a creamy brown
Your long mane is a midnight black
You run so fast, you don't touch the ground
I hope you come back
You never make me frown
But my reins are never slack
Sometimes with worry my head will pound
Then you make me laugh until I crack
I love you horse
Of course, of course

Brook Theis
Age: 9

Far past the hills
an Indian boy and his grandfather
gaze at the radiant sunset.
It looks as if Mother Earth
is trying to pry open the gateway
to Heaven by spitting up fireballs!
On the way back, the Moon Mother
beams upon them with her silvery glow
so they take the far, far journey home
to an ever-repeating meal of corn
and to fall into a relaxing sleep.

Taylor Jon Volkman

FEAST

F riends eating with you
E ating lots of food
A nd playing football
S urviving lots of food
T urkey gets greater and greater every year
    Feast!

Garrett Yost
Age: 9

MY BROTHER

My brother
Mean, but nice,
Cruel and hard,
But lovable too.

Sometimes I wish
I could sell him away
But then if I did,
Who would play with me?

Sometimes mean and impolite,
But I love him.
He's my brother
And he will always be in my heart.

Catherine Elizabeth Herrick
Age: 10

T hank your family
H appy families having joy
A nd having family over
N othing going wrong
K eep remembrance in our heart
S eeing family members
G iving hope
I ncluding others
V ery happy life
I nviting family members to eat
N eat house getting ready for company
G reeting people while coming in

Jenna Ogren
Age: 9

T hankful times
H appiness
A ttractive, enjoyable food
N obody alone
K ind people celebrate the birth of our country
S ome delicious food
G reat time to remember
I nvite people for a feast
V illages have parties
I n the ocean pilgrims sailed sixty-six days in and out
N othing but happiness for us all day
G iving love to everyone

Kayla Johnson
Age: 9

There are cougars here, there are cougars there.
　　There are cougars everywhere.
Some live in caves, some live in trees.
　　Some even live near cities.
But come from the east or come from the west.
　　At spotting cougars, the Canadians are the best.

Chris Wojtalewicz
Age: 10

J is for jack-o'-lanterns grinning in fright.
A t every street corner glowing with light.
C an they be real and alive as you?
K rackle-Snap go the candle flames.

O' h how they watch you when you walk by.

L istening closely to the sound of silence.
A nd everyone knows that they're all alive.
N obody dares to bother them.
T errific faces, scary faces.
E verywhere there's bright orange faces.
R unning wild in the pumpkin world.
N o one is missing their pumpkin on Halloween night.

David Kenneth Moore
Age: 10

SADNESS IN A BREEZE

I stand and feel a breeze blow by,
My brother's spirit it lifted up in the sky,
On he flies up to Heaven,
Now soaring to happiness,
And now my brother is free from pain,
As he soars and soars up to Heaven,
Now he sits with his Father and God,
My brother assures me that he is happy again,
He also tells me he will be with me forever,
And that he will always be in our hearts,
Where the sky is blue and grass is green,
Where the flowers stay in bloom for infamy,
Where all spirits will go forever and ever,
Some spirits are picked up quickly,
But some are picked up slowly
So we can say I love you and good-bye,
But we know that no matter how strong or weak
The breeze, we will always go to Heaven
With love in our hearts.

In loving memory of Glen Wilson

Jake T. Winckler
Age: 12

NAVY

Navy is our army that fights to be free
Navy is a gentle wave that flows with glee,
Navy is our flag that blows in the breeze
Navy is a bird that flies so swiftly.

The sound of navy is the winning of a war
The sight of a navy ship makes my heart soar,
When I think of navy I know I am free.
Navy is my jacket hanging on me.

Navy is a book that I just read,
Navy is my room that goes with my bed.
Navy is a flower floating in my pool.
Navy is a spruce tree at my school,

Navy is a map of our countryside
Navy is the ocean and the color of the tide,
Navy is my pencil I use every day.
Navy is a tear and the feeling of gay.

Faith D'Amato
Age: 10

BLUE

Blue is the color of the sky
The smell of the snow
On the mountain high.
Blue is the color when people die
It's also the color
Of mourners nearby.

Blue is the color of the sea
It's also the rain
That's falling on me.
Blue makes some people feel sad
But it does not me
It makes me glad.

Blue is the feeling of a cloud
The chirp of a bird
That is soft, not loud.
Blue is the color of my teacher's eyes
The one who helps me
Learn and be wise.

Blue is the color of a stream
Just like the one
I had in my dream.
Icy cold is water rushing overhead
It makes me want
To stay in my bed.

Michael Athens
Age: 10

I was affected
by a horrible attack
on September 11, 2001
it affected me
very many innocent people died on that day
there was an important person
her name was Barbara Olsen,
the secretary for the press
if I could do anything
better in our nation
it would to have the attack
on America
never happen
I feel that if one of my family members
had been on one of the flights
I would cry
and lock myself
in my room
I feel that this
is the most horrible thing
that happened in my life.

Samantha Roe
Age: 10

MY SHADOW

It is my twin
Mimics my every step
It appears out of nowhere
It's frozen 'til you move
I jump, it jumps
I wave, it waves
It sprawls up the wall,
And is there nice and tall,
My shadow is with me always.

Jennifer Lamphere
Age: 10

ANGEL

There is an angel in my classroom,
sitting next to me.
Helping me learn my answers,
for all of my A's and B's.

When I'm sitting in my classroom,
taking a math or spelling test,
I think about my angel
and a smile comes to me!

Who is this angel?
It's my teacher, can't you see!

Maia Henderson
Age: 9

AMERICA, THE BEST

The world is large,
But one place is best... America.

America started with thirteen colonies
And became fifty states... America.

America has a cool flag,
Gleaming with stars and red and white stripes
That stand for peace and harmony... America.

America's buildings are the best,
Some short, some tall.
We sleep, eat, shop, play,
And visit them... America.

America's parks are the best,
With their wonderful animals,
Mountain peaks, and trees... America.

The world is large,
but one place is best... America.

Lindsay Macdonald
Age: 9

REMEMBERING

Sometimes my heart is very sad
Because I miss my grandma so
I then remember the love she gave
And how she taught me to believe
My heart is happy once again

Todd Joseph Diamond

FRIENDSHIP

Friendship is like an iris,
it comes and goes quickly.

Friendship is sweet
like an iris.

When you have a friendship
you don't appreciate friendship.
But, when you are friendless
you miss friendship.

Friendship is the fertilizer
to our happiness.

Friendship is like an iris,
it goes and comes quickly.

Diane Sharp Kelly
Age: 11

AURORA AND DUSK

Caught in-between
a net of dying stars
and rich sunbeams.

I am not one,
but two
united at the hip.

In this arena,
one of fighting lights,
they sit in a gray suit.

Silver pillars
draped in black silk,
a lavender mosquito net blows in the wind.

The sun blasts heat rays
as the stars swing a black scepter.
Both blow kisses to their maidens, up above.

One sits in white satin,
golden hair pulled from her rosy lips,
wind making her butterfly wings flutter.

She is divine,
wearing gaudy colors,
prancing through the meadows: Aurora.

The other in black, webbed lace,
hair flung through a veil,
peeping over a pale face.

She is a crow in human form,
lips black and cracked,
ever hiding from light: Dusk.

So different,
yet so close,
dancing perfectly in the song of life.

How does one,
a person, a child,
live with this bitter sweet madness?

Neither smiling nor frowning
dancing nor crying,
just there.

I am my grandmother's sunshine,
my own torment;
Who am I?

I am me,
strengths and weaknesses
night and day.

I am part of strong Aurora
and of dim, nocturnal Dusk,
trapped in one single body.

My family's angel,
or a torn page in the book of light,
hidden by strong horizon lines.

Arianne Garcia
Age: 12

READING

I've been to the Alps
I've been to the desert
I've wielded a wand
and turned a witch into a fawn
I've flown through the air with great ease
and been on a flying trapeze
I've been 20,000 leagues under the sea
and been around the world in twenty-one days
and I've done all this by flipping a page!

James Bishop
Age: 11

GRADUATE

Leaving me here all by myself
Why does he have to go?
Will this end our relationship?
Him driving away,
will invite loneliness
to sit next to me at the dinner table.

Still I love him...
Congratulations Tommy!

Tiffany Johnson
Age: 12

MISTAKES

going to score
wrong way
a fantastic goal
wrong way
SCORE
wrong way
what!?!

Matt Rathbun
Age: 12

A LITTLE FUN

Once I had a little fun
I went to the beach where there was a lot of sun

I was hungry so I ate a delicious hot dog
And bready bun
I played and played in the sand a ton

Then I swam into the beach
Where I heard the lifeguard make a speech

He said I had to get out
The lifeguard called me a little sprout

Now it is the end of my little fun.
At the beach where there was a lot of sun

Rachel Fenn
Age: 7

TOKENS

In the arcade
lights
fun

people screaming.
Grandpa is playing with me and my brother.
A big smile across his face
he's enjoying it too.

I feel great
that he's having fun.

Before you know it
your time is up
"deposit more tokens"
flashes across the screen.
You feel mad because you were winning.

I wish that I could have inserted a token
and saved his life...

I also wish I could have
had a warning.

Garrett Ahern
Age: 12

DEATH

Death, comes to us all.
Death, beckons us down its hall.

Death, called and took my grandpa.

When I heard those fierce words

I felt like I would fall.
I felt like I was a torn-open doll.
I miss him...
don't we all.

Peter Hahn
Age: 12

THANK YOU

On this fine Thanksgiving day
This is what I'd like to say.
Thank you for my dancing feet
They help me run and tap a beat.

Thank you for my strong right hand
It helps me mold and play with sand.
Thank you for my eyes that see
Thank you for letting me be me!

Allison Chilewski
Age: 10

THE STORM

It was very, very cloudy.
I tried to run away.
But as soon as I took a step.
The sun came out to play!

Kali Malone
Age: 7

THANKSGIVING

A very strange thing happened
during Thanksgiving meal.
I have no clue if it was fake
or if it was real.
A UFO came out of space
and sucked up all our food.
Then dropped it down back in our plates
but I didn't eat it, I wasn't in the mood.
The drumsticks were disgusting,
the pie was problematic,
the rolls were rusting,
the stuffing was static.
Just when I thought that
my insides would erupt,
the UFO returned and out stepped --
I woke up!

Justin D. Schroeder
Age: 10

THE RAINBOW

The rainbow so pretty
  and so bright.
Bright, bright rainbow,
  please don't go.
If you go, then
  come pretty and bright again.

Patricia Olivas
Age: 8

GRANDPA

He walks out of the doctor's office,
sad
he has just me mortality
I get a phone call from his wife
our house fills with sorrow
we're powerless
we don't know what to do.
I wish that he could go back to when
he was well.
I wish this never happened.
Is this just a dream?
Will I ever wake up?
It can't be a dream it has gone on too long.

Cameron Henrikson
Age: 12

COLORFUL RAINBOWS

Rainbows are so colorful!
Pink, yellow, blue.
So bright and so beautiful.
Butterflies can be, too.

Brea Castillo
Age: 8

SNOWBOARDING

Riding down the mountain
  Carving the snow
How fast am I going
  Nobody knows.
Will I be able to stop
  I really hope so
I'm going to hit a ramp
  Oh, no! Oh, no!
I went really high
  If I fall I know
I'm going to break a bone
  Ow!
I'm coming down -- here I go
  I didn't land -- I roll -- roll -- roll
  Ahhhhh!
It hurts really bad
  I did break one of my wrist bones.

Michael D. Gonzales
Age: 13

RAIVEN

Ray-Ray is short for Raiven
She is as busy as a bee
And only twenty months
And knows every word in the book
She is spoiled rotten
She has little friends at her school
Named Tia and Chife
She is cute as a button.

Dawn Wattley

KISS IT GOOD-BYE

Standing at the plate
staring at the pitcher

waiting

the moment comes

you swing

you hammer the ball
jogging around the bases
hands stinging   .
when you touch home
you've got triumph on your face.

Eric Lippold
Age: 12

PEACE

I am hungry for peace
and I am thirsty for justice.
I am afraid
that one day
races will destroy
each other
because
we have not
gathered
to live together.

Nereida Montoya

FRIGHT NIGHT

You know what is really scary and mysterious
October 31, 2001.
The pumpkins are bright orange.
Scarecrows guard the cornfield.
Black cats looking out the window
of the haunted house with frightening eyes.
Someone just threw some dry ice
out the window to create fog.
Spiders make their webs
to catch their midnight snacks.
Vampires sharpen their teeth.
Witches get their pots ready and poof...
you are gone.

Tenisha A. Durán
Age: 10

ME MYSELF AND I

It's me myself and I.
It is not just me
myself and I.
I have my cousins
with me
and...
my
brothers
too.
It is not just
me
myself
and
I! I! I!
I'm happy it is not just
me myself and I!

Marshae Burton

LOVE

I love my family with all my heart;
They give me happiness, joy, and comfort;
When I am sad they make me feel happy.

Kevin Todd Blackmon Jr.
Age: 12

MOON AND STARS

Together you make a good pair
Not being together is very rare
Full moons sometimes give people a scare
But the stars make it seem fair
The clouds make the sky look bare
But the stars always shine through the air
That is why the moon and stars make a good pair.

Stephanie Nastick
Age: 13

WALKING WALKING AWAY

A family portrait,
A member missing,
Sadness everywhere,
Smiles in the past,
A broken heart,
A single rose,
A gravestone,
Walking walking away,
Nobody to replace,
Never the same again.

In memory of my Aunt Jean.

Adam Barnhart
Age: 12

THE FLOWER

I planted, I planted a beautiful flower
  and it was so little.
But one day in the morning,
  it grew as big as a giant.

Kelsey Espinoza
Age: 7

SKY

I like the sky
when the moon is glowing
and the clouds are growing

I like the sky
when the sky is getting darker
colored with a marker

I like the sky
when I am lying down
and I am falling asleep
is not a creep.

That is why
I like the sky.

Liliana Chavez

CRISPY COLORADO

Breeze and snow is where I'm from.
Cold wintertimes and snow-melting noons,
Hot chocolate nights and laughter around.
This is where I'm from and very proud.

The sweet sensation arose,
Summer was here,
Catching flies from the bush,
Which never let you down.
Being young you thought
They would taste like butter,
Too scared to try them,
You'd let them flutter.

These were the days you thought
You would never remember.
Raking the yard,
The pile would grow
It was time for slumber.
When suddenly,
Grandma's attic is what your nose tickled with.
Sinking,
Time was ticking,
The mess was still there.

Stuck in one place,
The world spins around,
Little girls in green, yellow, pink and blue,
Surrounded me as I drifted off to the moon.
My fingers glide on the surface of memories,
Comforting and over-used,
The reality appears.

Heidi Eckhoff
Age: 14

THANKSGIVING

By the time I saw the pumpkin
By the time I saw food
I didn't realize
But then I knew it was special
And then I knew it was Thanksgiving.

Lewis Flores
Age: 11

THE FISH

Once there was a fish.
He swam in a swish.
He was blue
And he knew how to chew.
That fish's name was Sue.

Colin J. Stein
Age: 7

The tragedy that happened
On September 11, 2001
Was disaster just beginning
Tears were shattered
Among the land
But our pride grew stronger
The terrorists came at us from above
Diving at the Twin Towers
With mighty powerful wings of steel
Crashing down the Twin Towers
Like claps of thunder
On a stormy night
Hearts were broken
And loved ones died
On this tragic day
But we need to remember
Our life before the tragedy

Kara Beane
Age: 10

SNOW

Snow, snow, snow
Snow can fall softly
Snow can melt slowly
Snow can be made into icy skates
Snow can be made into snowy men
Snow is fun
Snow is cool
Snow can be made into snowy faces
Snow is cold
Snow rules!
Snow, snow, snow

Morgan Talmage
Age: 8

SNOW

Stars falling from a luminous sky
Land safely and protect anything
And everything on earth.
A soft layer of untouchable diamonds
Creates a mirage,
One that cannot be touched or kept forever,
But returns each year.
The feeling of love and beauty,
However cold,
Contains infinite inner warmth.
A speck of freedom in a vast world of captivity.

Elena Harman
Age: 14

MY GREAT-GRANDMA!

It's late
at night
when I'm
getting ready
for bed
we get
a phone
call it's
the hospital
my dad
starts to
cry and
that's the
first time
I've seen
him cry
Then he
hangs up
I say
what's the matter
he takes
a deep
breath and
says your
grandma's gone
what do you mean
she died
I cry
and I
don't stop.

Jessica Troxell

When I was jumping in the leaves,
I found some in my sleeves.
Then I found it in my hair,
And I looked around it was everywhere.
Then I saw my friends,
And I didn't want it to end.

Cory Smith

Chelsea,
Reader, smart, tough, athletic
Sister of Amber
Lover of books, our dog, our family
Who feels happy when she gets her way,
Angry when she's in trouble,
Sad when her feelings are hurt
Who fears kidnappers, the dark, the devil
Who would like to see a dead person,
Monkeys, wild horses
Resident of the state of Illinois
Diggs

Amber Diggs
Age: 10

QUIT IT

Making weird noises
and laughing a lot
when here comes the teacher
and she said
    "Quit It"
Talking to my neighbor
and leaning back in my chair
when here comes the teacher
and she said
    "Quit It"
I'm falling out of my chair
and laughing quite a bit
when here comes the teacher
and she said
    "Quit It"
I was sitting in my chair
minding my own business
when here comes the teacher
and guess what she said
    "Good Job"

Nick Brant

SMELLS FROM THE KITCHEN

When I came home from school
I smell something so divine
so delectable with taste
it makes my mouth water.
    Smells from the kitchen.
I follow the smell
like a hound dog
rushing to the source
then I see croissants
from ground to ceiling
cinnamon rolls rolling
around me like a floating
cloud of heaven.
    Smells from the kitchen
Doughnuts bulging with frosting and sprinkles
animal marzipan floating in the air
peeps peeping around me,
hey wait a minute
this feels like a dreeeeeeeaam
    Smells from the kitchen

Max Afshar

SOOTY

My dear cat
sneezing his way to death.

My mom and I head to the airport
on our journey to Seattle.

My dad waves good-bye
while I see my poor little cat
sitting in the window.

We arrive at the airport in Seattle
and take a cab to our hotel.

An hour later our phone in our room rings
my cat has died. I no longer have a cat
to sit on my bed or love in my heart.

I love you Sooty

Matthew E. Otto

PEEPA

He had white hair,
like any grandpa should,
I loved him,
like any granddaughter should

He was sick
Alzheimer's disease
and old age

One day
during the end of the school year,
I learned he was gone

I can't remember now,
If I cried,
I just remember the
sting of loss.

Even now,
thinking of him,
tears come to my eyes

He loved me
and I loved him
in the balance of nature

Peepa,
I'll never forget him.

Never

Casey Delanoy

I am Homo sapiens
Sapiens
I made jewelry
And necklaces
And anything else we had
Years ago
We made clothes

Anthony A. Jue

If I were a Beaufort scale three,
I'd have a gentle breeze flowing through the sky.
I'd have a force of wind
from 8 to 12 miles per hour.
I'd have a taste like a winter fresh mint.
My sound would be soft as silk.
I'd drift through the air like a feather.
My breeze would be cool like sprinkling rain.
I'd be the discovery of wonderful.

Brianna Broe
Age: 10

C ool
A dorable
T houghtful
I nteresting
E verything

She's always there when I need her.
She is the very best.
Her brown eyes deep as honey
and oh so gentle.
Sometimes it is hard to believe
that Catie and I aren't sisters.
We have been through everything
but now being the best of friends
since fourth grade
in fifth grade something happened
we were split up.
One in one class one in the other
now we're different people
I mean we're always different people
but for a while
Carie and Catie were the same people
never saw one for the other.
It was best. I long for those days
Catie and Carie together forever.

Carie Stamp

MOONLIGHT

Moonlight flowing,
A soft river of Paradise

Shifting,
Swirling,
Drifting off into the night,

Moonlight flowing,
A soft river of Paradise,

Leaving a trail of milky white light,
Floating off into the night,

Moonlight flowing,
A soft river of Paradise,

Misty and bright,
Full of cool,
Soft,
Light,
Oh
What a sight...

Moonlight

Isabella Marie Shaw

EAGLES

Eagles
golden flashes
flying, soaring, diving
gliding powerfully through air
Freedom

Colin W. Loughe
Age: 9

STARS

Gazing,
soaring
among the stars.

I fly past
millions of tiny beads
on a safety pin.

Diving,
The stars seem to write
on the sky
as if it were a giant blackboard.

I swoop,
landing on the moon.
Gaze at the world, where the sun
peaks over the blue crimson sky.

Alexandra Wollum

HALLOWEEN

Halloween
It comes once a year
Yelling trick-or-treat

Halloween
Candy in my pillowcase
Running through the night

Halloween
Jack-o'-lanterns glowing
Bright into the night

Halloween
Monsters and mimes
The breeze chills your spine

Halloween
Organs playing themselves
Screaming people you always meet
Lights flashing on your street.

Halloween
Midnight comes it's all over
Except the fun!

Halloween

Mac Cassin

HOCKEY

H ard hits
O ffense and defense
C hecking
K nockouts
E aston equipment
Y outh leagues

Wilson S. Marlin
Age: 10

THE BEACH IN MEXICO

A warm sunny day at the beach,
I smell the salty sea water
as I jump the huge waves,
I taste the strong salty water
in my mouth,
I can touch the crispy sand in my hands,
I see the bright colorful sunset
gleaming in the sky
making a shadow in the sea,
I hear the sea gulls cawing for food
and the waves roaring in my ears.

Camille D. Shoemaker
Age: 10

SNOW

Snow falling,
Sleds spinning,
Whirling winds,
Bone shivering coldness.

Snow falling,
Sipping hot chocolate,
Playing a game,
Gazing,
At the snow.

Snow falling,
Building a snowman,
Taking a carrot,
Building a nose,
Completing a mouth,
With small little balls.

Snow falling,
More snow,
More snow,
And more snow.

Thad Walker

SNOW

The cold snow coming down
When I catch a snowflake
It tastes so gross
It makes my mouth feel cold
As an icicle

The snow is cold and makes me
Get the chills
The snow does not smell like anything
I can imagine it sounds
Like a cracking firework
As it is going to explode!

Nicole Vizas
Age: 10

THE SUN

Sun
hot, red
shining, burning, flaming
sunrise, sunset, sky, ball
gleaming, orbiting, glowing
cold, white
Moon

Henry H. Hoyt
Age: 10

MY TEACHERS' NAMES

Elizabeth
My teacher's name is Elizabeth she is a great
Teacher Elizabeth is the best teacher she was
Born in 1972.

Sonny
Sonny is a great teacher he was born in the 1977
Sonny helps me with my work.

Amy
Amy is a great teacher she was born in the 1955
And she is so nice
I don't know how to describe her.

MacKenzie Schledorn - Rudden

TERRORISM

Just the thought of it blows my mind.
The people that did this weren't very kind.
But why this peaceful place?
I wonder as I pace.
Maybe this was in the course of fate.
Or was it just hate?
I see tears run down many faces,
As I tie my shoelaces.
It is off to school I go.
And I ask myself who is a friend and who is foe?

Brett S. Porterfield

KINDNESS

Kindness rings
Laughter sings

Kindness is as gentle as a kitten
Kindness is like a playful pup
Kindness is as sweet as a box of chocolates
Kindness is a good friend

Kindness sings
Laughter rings

Laughter is as bright as a shiny star
Laughter is like puppies rolling around
Laughter is as sweet as a chocolate chip
Laughter is in a good friend

Kindness rings
Laughter sings

Katy Rininger
Age: 10

WINTER

The snow spills from sky,
Over frosty grass and ponds,
It lies on the ground,
Like a lifetime of playing,
Snow awakens the whole world.

Kongpeng Tommy Lor
Age: 9

MY FAVORITE PLACE

On an autumn day
With buzzing bees
I sit beneath.
The apple trees
　In my favorite place.

I sink into
The golden leaves
And stare up at the pattern
The branches weave.
　In my favorite place.

Above my tree
The sky is blue
The orchard prepares
For autumn new.
　In my favorite place.

Hope Broyles
Age: 10

COLORS

The sun is yellow
like a happy fellow.
The grass is green
like a beautiful stream.
The sky is blue
like my love is true.

Marisol Zamora
Age: 13

BOO

This one day of the year
where scary things appear
BOO!!

All of the parks all today
where little kids go and play
BOO!!

Candy overflowing bags
while scary goblins come and beg
BOO!!

Max Corra
Age: 10

AMERICA COMES TOGETHER

They thought they could break us,
  But we have grown strong.
We come together
  to protect the good
  and demolish the wrong.

On that tragic morning,
  none of those people wanted to die.
After it all
  our flag still flies high.

Now, everyone's favorite heroes
  are Batman, Superman and Ninjas no more.
It's our firefighters, police,
  and rescue workers we adore.

Let us bring justice
  to our foes.
May God bless us all.
Let us bring terrorism
  to its fall.

Katelyn Koch
Age: 12

AMERICA

The A ll-American dream
The M en and women defending our nation
The E xcellent government that keeps America running
The R ed, white and blue
    The men and women who lost their
  L I ves September 11
The C ountry that I love above the rest
The A lways-ready-to-fight-back nation

America, the beautiful
  America, the strong
    America, the country that to me does no wrong.

Amanda Gonzales
Age: 13

OOPS

After art class, passing the time,
I still don't know what possessed my mind.
I walked over to the microwave; I pushed a button.
I didn't know something would happen
If in the microwave there was nuttin'.
Next thing I know, I'm in a lot of trouble.
And it seems I've burst everyone's bubble.
But, I learned a very valuable lesson,
With buttons and radiation,
I will never again be messin'.
I'm sorry.

Danz Martinez
Age: 12

BABY-SITTING

She's yelling and screaming
Stop her please, quick.

Oh gross, please make her stop
She's making me sick.

Oh no, don't do that
I can't believe she threw that.

I'm done I can't do it
Baby-sitting, I'm so through with it.

Audrey Goodman
Age: 11

LIFE

Life is a great thing.
   Every step you take is LIFE.
Everything you do or see is LIFE.
   Just live LIFE for the best,
      and pray for the best.
Don't take advantage of life.
   Love life.
You don't know what's going to happen next.

Bonnie Rae Olguin
Age: 12

YOUR HEART

A heart is filled with life.
A mind is filled with memories of your life.
A heart is filled with joy and happiness.
A mind is like a friend that will never tell a secret.

Louis Archuleta
Age: 11

AMERICA

Red is for the anger felt
   for all the people who were killed.

White is for the color of the faces
   of the people who were scared
   of what this person's heart was filled.

Blue is for the sky
   that is now turned gray.

The stars are for the free will
   that God gave us
   to do what we may.

And the flag is for what unity is
   because we are all in this together --
All for one and one for all.

Cara O'Connor
Age: 12

I WISH

I wish everybody had a nice cozy bed.
I wish I had magical powers.
I wish everything was free for everybody.
I wish my family could live forever.

Anna Luisa Delarosa
Age: 10

PIGSTY

My room is a pigsty
It never gets clean.
My room is a pigsty
It should never be seen.

My room is a pigsty
I should blow up my room.
My room is a pigsty
I should blow it up soon.

My room is a pigsty,
But it's not all that bad,
So if there is nothing to add
About my pigsty room
Then I should pick it up
Before it goes
BOOM!

Shannon MacDonnell
Age: 10

FALL

Fall autumn same season same weather.
Crisp breeze
  Warm day
    Fresh air
      Sunny sky
Fall autumn same season same weather.

Autumn fall same colors.
Red
  Green
    Brown
      Orange
       Yellow
Autumn fall same colors.

Fall autumn same things to see.
Dry grass
  Crunching leaves
    Bare trees
      Prickly grass and rough and broken leaves.
Fall autumn same thing to see.

Johanna Serrano
Age: 11

EAGLE

Eagle
air predator
mother gets food for kids
Eagles are flying predators.
Eagles

Rachel Marcellus
Age: 8

HOBO DAN

There once was a hobo named Dan,
who slept in a garbage can,
one day he woke up,
in the back of a garbage truck,
and now he's a garbage man.

He drives by every week,
collecting all the trash,
his clothes are started to reek,
and his face is covered in ash.

I feel sorry for old Hobo Dan,
who used to sleep in our garbage can,
until he woke up,
in a smelly garbage truck,
and now he's the local garbage man.

Tyler Gilbert
Age: 13

STRESS

As homework holds me down,
My mind tries desperately to get away,
It only finds locked doors.
I feel like I'm drowning in an ocean of stress.
I try to swim to the top for air.
But the current leads me back down
To the evil cage of the deep.
I scream for help,
but voice doesn't come out.
Stress is taking over my life,
for now I am its servant.
Darkness and gloom is the only thing I see.
I feel dying hot, yet chilly and cold.
A little bit of freedom is all I ask.
Just a glitter of hope.
Wait...
Is that a light?

Kendra Jones
Age: 11

NIGHTTIME

Alone in the darkness,
Still alone in the light.
Wondering what defines daytime,
And what defines night.

Is it because at night,
All the villains come out.
And they hang around town,
Just walking about.

They'll commit their crimes,
Then run away.
Just to come back,
At the end of the next day.

Or is it because at night,
You're alone in your bed.
Thinking of something,
Your ex-best friend said.

And as one lonely tear,
Falls from your eye,
You wonder,
Since when did I cry?

Since when did I let my problems,
Get in my way.
Since when did I cry,
At the end of the day.

But then you realize this one tear is familiar,
This one tear you know well.
You just hide it during the day,
So that no one can tell.

But at night,
All your emotions come out.
While outside the villains,
Are walking about.

Mary Morr
Age: 11

There once was an elephant from Spain,
Who always fell asleep on the train.
Then the train came to a stop
And the elephant went kerplop
Then the elephant poured down rain.

Taylor Rebecca Jordan

NEON GREEN

A flashing sign outside the door
Moving silent but fast from person to person
Grabbing at their eyes
Like a bird grabbing at a French fry
Matching the fast moving skin-tight clothing
As it dances in the club
Bringing back the dead
The eighties
Moving like the smooth electronic
High-pitched music
Sending the smell of lime juice throughout the club
It is turned off
Few things remain
The sound of a bee hovering in your mind
The smell of electricity hovering
Around the sign's smooth glassy outline
And a small flame burning
Always remembering the fallen trends of the past

Clayton Kenney
Age: 14

POLAR BEAR FUZZ

I discovered a new color today.
I realized I was drinking Polar Bear Fuzz
In the form of chai tea.
Not just any chai tea, however.
Chai tea with one grain short of enough sugar,
And milk until it overflows.
Yes, I know that Polar Bear Fuzz
Is not really a color,
In your mind.
But it is
In mine.
It can't be drawn or painted or copied,
And is not to be confused with white or off-white
Or yellow or tan.
The only way is to turn one lucky polar bear's fur
Into ink for a moment,
Just long enough to have him roll over
On the sheet,
Making a dense, thick cloud of eggnog
That goes much deeper than the paper.
So I guess it isn't really a color,
Just a river of eggnog mist,
With a yellowish glow
And burn marks from the sun.

Alyssa Pluss
Age: 15

WINTER

Winter, is very cold.
All the rain turns to ice.
It's war inside my house.
On the news that night
It said it was going to snow
A little bit of frost.
But I came to realize
I was lost.
Nowhere to be found.
There I was covered in the freezing snow.
In the forest nowhere to go.
No one could have survived.
In the freezing snow.
Lie a baby.
Crying in its sleep.
I say awaken little baby.
So I took her with me.
You couldn't believe it
I found my way home.

Olivia Martinez
Age: 10

OUR FLAG

Working hard side by side
Looking at the waving flag
The red, white, blue as if it
Were saying God bless you

Julia Rhoden
Age: 11

FAITH

The confidence in someone
The belief and trust in another person
The confidence in doing something
A religious belief
You got to have faith

Paul M. Lehan
Age: 13

IN MY HEART

When summer goes to winter,
When today changes to tomorrow,
When a week goes to year --
You are here in my heart.

When day changes to night,
When loud goes silent,
When peace changes to war --
You are still --
Going to be here in my heart.

When death becomes me,
When I become death,
When all has passed --
You will still be here...
In my heart.

In loving memory of my father,
Anselmo Elifaz Honorio Vialpando.

Nicole Vialpando
Age: 14

BLUE MARKER

Blue makes me feel like I'm standing
On the bright and shiny moon,
Thinking of nothing but the stars
And how they are made.

Then it makes me feel like a blue lake
That is reflecting the sun
With a flock of blue jays just waiting for it to rain.
That is what blue reminds me of.

Samantha Wiseman
Age: 10

MY CAT THE BRAT

As   black
As the   night. As
smooth as the stream. As weird as it
may   seem.   Some-
times happy sometimes sad, some-
times you make my other cat really,
really mad. You can be sweet and
sometimes sour. I have to check
on you every other hour. So
when I look at you, I will
think then say, "Why
haven't I yelled
at you
today?"

Crystal Peduzzi
Age: 13

SO FAR AWAY

Sparkle, Sparkle
In the sky
Oh why Oh why
Can't I fly?
To the moon
With a spoon
As I left the
Sand dune
Wearing
Fruit of the Loom
Listening to the tune of a baboon
In my cocoon,
I sprouted and bloomed
Around noon
I SHOT
To the moon,
With my Big Balloon!
So now I can rest,
For I've done my BEST!

Ashleigh Janell Bohman
Age: 13

NOCTURN

Night is black, night is dark
This is the time to see a star
I am going to wish on you
Star light star bright
I wish...

Kristen Emanuelson
Age: 6

FLOWERS

Flowers need air.
Flowers need food.
Flowers need water like me and you.
Flower are like humans:
Humans are like flowers.
Flowers are beautiful like Jesus Christ and you.

Nicole Gonzales

I REMEMBER...

I can remember your smell,
Your eyes
And the fun we had together.

You had to go hunting
That accident had to occur the next day.

I can remember you kept coming back,
The night before.

That duck had to come in sight,
You had to shoot it.

I remember the call we got,
Telling us what had happened.

You had to go get the duck,
In the icy cold water.
That's when it happened,
The sharp pain in the middle
Of your heart.

You had a heart attack
And you were gone.

Alyson Garrett
Age: 12

AMERICA

The people walk quickly
cell phones ring
the click of bright red heels
business men with black briefcases
eating fast-food meals

then suddenly a big BOOM

like a bird high in the sky
the fire, smoke and tragedy
take everyone by surprise

but, we soon recover
and know our enemy can't smother
our PRIDE

WE ARE AMERICANS!

Angela Rodgers
Age: 11

SHARING SORROW

It's odd
How you don't want to cry,
But the feeling is too strong
And the tears overflow.

I was tensely sitting in my music room
Talking quietly to my music teacher.

The tough conversation turned to things
That pinch at my pride.

I tried not to cry ~

So hard, I tried!

I almost died,
And I could not stop.
The tears
They fell softly down my cheeks.
She cried, too.
She cried with me.
Me, her, we cried.

She told me,
That I should not hide
My worries deep inside.

That is the time
I felt like I knew her
Better than I ever have.

She told me
I should not be afraid
To share my troubles.

If you read this poem
Then what I have to say to you,
Is neither should you.

Michelle Richardson
Age: 13

SMILEY FACES

Smiley faces are
Smiley faces are blue
Smiley faces are pink
Smiley faces are purple too!
Smiley faces are on erasers
Smiley faces are on hats
Smiley faces are on markers
Smiley faces are on cats!
Smiley faces can be anywhere
Smile faces can be in your hair!
Smiley faces can be in your food
Smiley faces can affect your mood!
Smiley faces are
Smiley faces are blue
Smiley faces are pink
Smiley faces are purple too!

Jennifer Abamonte
Age: 11

GYMNASTICS

Gymnastics is cool
You flip and rope climb
You do hand stands.
Gymnastics once a week
Is not enough for me!

Alexandrea Harris
Age: 7

WHY?

Why do things happen the way they do?
Why do people do such horrible things to each other?
Why do bad things happen to good people?
Why must people die because of others?
Why are people poor and rich?
Why does money mean so much to people?
Why must people be jealous of others?
Why did God let this happen?
Why do tragedies happen?
Why does life always go the wrong way?
Why did so many people die in the national tragedies?
Why?

Aimee Martinez
Age: 11

BEING ALL ALONE

Alone can be reading a book,
  or taking a fish off a hook.
Alone can be picking a flower,
  or being trapped inside a tower.
Alone can be taking a walk,
  or drawing a picture with some chalk.
Alone can be looking at a shooting star,
  or trying to figure out who you are.
Alone can be visiting an enchanted place,
  or drifting off into outer space.
Alone can be listening to church bells ring,
  or swinging high up in a swing.
Alone can be asleep in wonderland,
  or playing dump trucks in the sand,
Alone can be eating candy galore,
  or petting a kitten whom you adore.
Alone can be waiting at a train station,
  or trying to use your imagination.

Kayli Zahller
Age: 11

WATER

A river is like a ribbon
Curving through the land
Flowing ever onward
Over rocks and sand

The river feeds the ocean
Its water blue and deep
Some say the salty ocean
Came from tears that angels weep

The sun draws ocean vapor
High into the air
The vapor forms wispy clouds
That float freely through the air

The clouds carry their heavy burden
Far across the land
Before releasing pouring rain
That falls down onto parched sand

Nick Gray
Age: 14

Flowers are really mellow
and usually bright yellow.

They stay in the same place all day
and sway in a unique way.

They are good to give to females,
Followed up by sensitive e-mails.

You type them up so quick and dandy,
When female receive them it's just like candy.

Flowers are beautiful just like you and me,
I will love you forever.

So, forever it shall be.

Jeffery Englund
Age: 13

MY DAD

My dad likes to watch TV.
He watches TV more than me.
He likes to watch the news and sports.
And likes to sit there eating tortes.
He can watch from two to ten and won't get sleepy.
This is the story of my dad and TV.

Carlos Peralta
Age: 11

A HERO IN DISGUISE

My mom is a hero in disguise
She has a red cape and laser beam eyes
She has a harm detector
She is the world's protector
She can fly in the air
She can do any dare
She can cook a good meal
She understands how I feel
She can be funny
She can fix a hurt tummy
She can perfectly tuck me into bed
She can fix hurt imaginary Ted
My mom is a hero in disguise
My mom has changed many people's lives

Celene Doyle
Age: 13

THANKSGIVING

Thanksgiving so great.
On Thanksgiving we eat lots.
Good old Thanksgiving.

Keili Clive Foster

THINGS I'VE WANTED TO BE

I've wanted to be a doctor, maybe a plastic surgeon
I've wanted to be a bird, more specifically a pigeon
I've wanted to be a horse trainer, a dolphin trainer too
I've wanted to work with animals at the Denver Zoo

I want to be a lawyer with cases in a court
I want to be an actress who isn't very short
I want to be a chef and make pies
   like cherry and key lime
I think I'll be an actress in a TV show
   with lawyers and cook in my free time

Laura Bingert
Age: 14

ONE LITTLE SOUL

One little soul,
Two little souls,
Three little souls,
One hundred little souls,
Two hundred little souls,
Three hundred little souls,
How many souls?
Too many souls.

How could all these souls delay all,
How come?
How?
Why?
When?
Where?
Why are all souls betraying me?

Just for another soul,
To have,
To hold,
To carry,
Forever.
How come?

All the little souls dancing around,
All the little souls smelling pansies,
All the little souls,
Coming, coming,
Every single soul goes he-ha, he-ha.

Tonight, my soul and I will go forever,
And ever, and never come back.
To the great garden,
'Til the end of time.

One little soul goes bye-bye, bye-bye,
Two little souls say bye-bye,
One hundred little souls say bye-bye, bye-bye.
Say good-bye.

Tabitha Klataske
Age: 11

GOD BLESS AMERICA

We are all one
we stand hand in hand.
Although we run,
we do not hide.
We show our fear
with a cry and a tear.
When we look
we see one country,
not many.
So, God bless America
for we show our concern.
Even though our lives were burned,
we show our love in an eye,
in a cry,
but we stand as one --
not many!

Travis Fantozzi
Age: 11

FRIENDS

They'll jump on the bed with you
to sing with a microphone brush,
They'll give you the latest scoop
on your current crush,
They let you borrow everything,
even their expensive new skirt,
They'll be the one you can lean on
when you're hurt,
Together, you'll be the mall's most frequent guests,
They'll give you the answers
to tomorrow morning's big test,
They'll stay up late with you,
laughing and giggling all night,
They'll help you stick up for what's right,
They'll ignore the crabbiness,
They'll join in the silliness,
They'll turn your frowns upside down,
They'll shop with you
'til you find the perfect gown,
They'll understand
the "I don't feel like talking" moods,
They'll be the greatest partner for scoping out dudes,
They'll help during the hard circumstances,
They'll push you to take chances,
They'll celebrate the really great stuff,
They'll know when you've had enough,
They'll understand the stories
that need to be shared relentlessly,
And together, you'll put the "e" in "We"
...TRUE FRIENDS ARE THE BEST!!!

Chelsea Strickland
Age: 14

HEAVEN

You're the closest thing to Heaven
I will ever touch
The soft sounds of your whispers
are what I love so much
The way you're always there
like the shadow by my side
The security of your hand in mine
I'd never try to hide
The strength of your arms
holding me tight
The warmth of your love
could warm the darkest night
The stars sprinkled in your eyes
glow inside my heart
And my greatest fear
is us growing apart
So promise to never leave me
and I will do the same
Never let go
You're the closest to Heaven I've ever come

Corie Robertson
Age: 14

SING

If you sing
It will bring
Joy to all
In spring and fall.

If you dance
People will give you a glance.
It will be
The same if you sing.

If you now
Go out and sing
You will see
What joy you bring.

Morgan Falls
Age: 10

A CLEAR NIGHT DRIVE

On a clear night, go for a drive
You must have a convertible to make it worthwhile
The weather must be warm, not too warm,
A cool breeze must tingle your nose
When you step outside
Now you can Drive...
Look at the sights
Especially the stars and moon
Identify constellations
If you know none, make your own
Feel the cool breeze slide through you --
Watch your clothes rustle in the wind
Lean on your head out the side
And wait for a divine drink of the night's
Blue juice of heaven
With crystals of salt and a slice of wondrous life

Ari Leventhal
Age: 16

MUSIC

M usic is the best.
U nresistable.
S ee you in music.
I hope you go to music.
C ome to music.

Taylor Bain
Age: 8

SPRINGTIME

Spring is a time of joy;
A time of fun.

Spring is a boy
That tans in the sun.
Spring is a girl
That found a squirrel when she twirled.

Spring is a tree
That blows in the breeze;
As if it is frightened
By some bees.

Brittany Alexandra Gilbert
Age: 10

I AM FROM

I am from the swings in the park,
the lights in the city.

I am from the mall,
musicals, and Broadway shows.

I am from my grandpa's laugh,
and the chuckle of his belly.

I am from the tip of a speeding boat
bounding over the waves,
from the warm sand on the beach,
from the red sunset,
and from the mist of the waves.

I am from my sister's giggle,
and her smile.

I am from the posters,
I am from rings,
I am from laughs.

I am from stories
that will last a lifetime.

Blair Weigum
Age: 12

KLMS

Kiani is first name
Kittens are her favorite
Kiani kisses her mom
Kiani like kites.

Loves her sister
Loves lions
Likes to be daring and brave
Leaves are fun she thinks.

Monkeys sound funny
Many things she likes
Money is what she wants
Mittens are cold to her.

Soccer is her game
She loves her family
She loves shortcuts
Smiles are very cool to her.

Kiani Stutz
Age: 8

GYMNASTICS

Gymnastics, gymnastics
What a great game.
Gymnastics, gymnastics
I even love your name.

I love all the tumbles and flipping and bars,
Someday my friends and I may even be stars.

The tumbles are fun,
The flipping is great,
I wish I could stay at gymnastics so late.

Gymnastics, gymnastics,
What a great game,
But my mom is calling my name!
It's time to go inside to get ready for bed,
I hope you had as much fun as I did!

Stacey Sims
Age: 11

REMEMBERING

I remember,
   her cancer slowly getting worse
   and her strange sudden loss of hair
   supposedly could help somehow.
I remember,
   being called to the hospital that morning,
   the sound of her choked gasps for breath,
   as she struggled to stay alive.
I remember,
   all the weeping faces,
   and the feelings of anguish and loss
   as tears ran down my face.
I remember,
   her face becoming paler,
   as her spirit left her body
   and departed from this world.

Sara Jelinek
Age: 13

GRANDMA

When I think of you
I see you smiling,
making me laugh.
Telling me how
much you love me,
holding me close.
I didn't see it coming
but when it did,
the tears started running.
It was like a flash of light,
you were gone so fast.
I wish that I could've
been with you.
Boy am I going to miss you!
I will never forget
the memories we shared.
Good-bye Grandma...

Jenna Garcia
Age: 13

SNOWFALL

Snowflakes falling,
gently landing,
twirling, twirling.
hot cocoa sipping,
scalding hot,
slurp, slurp.
Snowman building,
freezing cold,
pat, pat,
oh this winter
wonderland.

Krista Coulter
Age: 11

If I were a Beaufort scale number five,
I would tug at flags and blow people's hats
off their heads.
I'd make dogs bark, leaves flutter, and doors rattle.
I'd make timber fly through the air,
waves tumble onto the beach,
and trees sway to-and-fro.
I would feel like cold rain striking your face
and be strong like the king of the world.
I'd soar all over the planet visiting many different
places and seeing many different things.
Then I would dash back home to where I was born.
I'd die down to a breeze and then fade away.

Juliana Rose Nicole

YOU CAN MAKE A DIFFERENCE

You can make a difference.
You can light the fire.
You can change the hearts of millions,
If that is your desire.

You can share the love of God,
If it lies within.
You can let your light shine bright,
Or cover it with sin.

You can take the challenge,
Or give the chance away.
But your time is running out,
Through the passing of each day.

You can grow a flower
With just one little seed.
Love and determination,
Is all that you will need.

So try to make a difference,
And you will light the fire.
In the hearts of millions
And make it their desire.

Rebecca Gunther

OCEAN JOURNEY

A ll of the creatures of the
B eautiful sea
C onnect to the
D aring shark, crab, and the
E el.
F ish
G racefully swim
H appily together.
I nside the aquarium I learned that
J ellyfish have tentacles.
K nowing this, I will never touch one.
L obsters live in the ocean also.
M onsters, also known as sharks,
N est.
O ctopus are very large, yet can fit in
P laces the size of your fist. You must never
Q uake by a shark or it may attack you.
R unning would not be very easy
   to do in the water
S o you should swim
T owards the shore very quickly.
U nder the water lie many interesting life forms.
W aves bring sea life close to the shore at dusk.
e X tremely large mammals, such as the whale,
   teach their
Y oung to swim and survive by
Z igzagging through the ocean water.

Ashley Soliday
Age: 12

GRANDAD

You were here once,
But now you are gone,
But, you're still close to my heart.

I see you in my memory,
And laugh!
We never thought...

We never thought I'd never see you again,
Sitting upon your chair,
Reading a book or telling a story.

Oh to hear one more story,
Those stories were the best,
To hear you tell a story,
Oh what I would give!

And when I go and sit upon your chair,
I feel you so close around me,
And oh it feels so grand!

Or to go into your garage,
And smell the smell,
I think of what used to be...

Megan Concannon
Age: 11

If I were a category one hurricane
I would sweep through towns
bending trees and stealing the gentlemen's hats.
I would taste like a backyard garden
of dirt and grass
as I whip at your face at 75 miles per hour.
I would feel powerful
like a wolf howling at the moon.
I would sound like a bugling elk screaming
and wailing under the light of the stars.
I would smell of earth and greenery
like a recently rained on woodland.
I would wash up 45-foot waves
to pound on the property of coastal homes.
The warm water from the ocean would feed me
so my whirling winds could swirl even faster.
Sometimes, I would gently carry things in my arms
for miles without breaking them.
After I had fulfilled my duty as a hurricane,
I would dump all my water like a clumsy child
dropping a dozen jumbo Ping-Pong balls.
Then I would slowly fade away,
leaving my damage and wreckage behind.
Because, Mother Nature
can't be stopped.

Amelia Kucic
Age: 8

If I were a Beaufort 12
I would send cars soaring into the wind
like pieces of notebook paper.
I would rip roofs from homes
and hurl playhouses out of yards.
I would tug trees from their roots
like pulling weeds from a garden.
I'd make stop signs dangle from their poles.
Windows would break
and flags would tear in my path.
I would send books from their shelves
and stuffed animals would fly
like birds from their holes.
I'd fling kitchen utensils
through the air like airplanes.
And if you were wearing a hat,
I'd send it through the wind like a roof shingle
as I blew water across the street.

Austin W. H. Holmes
Age: 9

WASHIN' DIRTY DISHES

Imagine the foul smell of day-old, dirty dishes,
Just waiting to be washed,
Sitting comfortably in the sink,
Resting peacefully,
Waiting to be touched and cared by fragile hands.
They enjoy looking up at you,
Just admiring what you do to them...
You take one fragile, dirty dish into your hands,
And you caress it, you take pride
In wiping that dish so that all the build-up
On the dish becomes a fresh clean smile.
You take that clean dish and you carefully place it
On the rack to be dried and be set on display
Before being used again.
Then you glance at one more dish that you forgot;
It was hiding in the corner of your eye,
Hoping that you will wash it
To make it fresh yet again.
You then repeat the process
And you dip it in the water,
Glance at it through the suds,
Smiling, you pick it up with happy hands,
Making it smile at you.
You wipe that dirt-infested sponge
And you swipe that dish so vigorously
To gradually start to see yourself
Appearing in the dish while whistling to yourself
And making up new songs and reciting it
To your faceless dishes silently applauding.
You finally finish that last, spotless, smiling dish,
And you place it carefully into the rack.

You walk away, and for some reason,
You turn around, and glance back
At your finished, clean dishes, and you realize
That your happy, spotless dishes
Are looking at you and smiling at you,
Grateful for your obligation to clean them
When they're dirty, and take pride in doing it...
You're no longer washin' dirty dishes,
You're washin' masterpieces of colorful art.

Aaron Green
Age: 14

WINTER

The winter is cold.
Cold, frosty, freezing, breezy,
Jump into the snow,
Fun sledding with family,
Wonderful snowing winter.

Walter Carl Schlosser
Age: 8

WHEN I DREAM

Floating on a cloud up in the sky,
Bathing in a magic pool,
Gliding through a golden mist,
Sliding on a slide of silver,
Flying through a mist of dreams,
Swimming through a magic blue,
Is it true?

Elizabeth Schyling
Age: 7

I am a Australopithecus afarensis
3.9 million years ago
I eat
I sleep
I find food
I am Lucy
The Australopithecus afarensis
That got dug up by Donald Johansen
And now I am embalmed
In a museum

Matthew Yee Westfall

FAMILY

Family has love
Friendship
Family has giveness
And forgiveness
That is what
Family is!!

Amanda Trujillo
Age: 12

DRAMA

Drama is great.
Drama is exciting.
Drama is smiling, laughing and crying.
Drama shows feeling;
Drama shows emotion
  like the part in "Twelfth Night"
  that takes place on the ocean.

Valerie Anne Medina
Age: 12

ANIMALS

A
B uffalo
C an
D ance
E nthusiastically.
F lying
G eese
H onk.
I mpalas
J ump
K indly
L ying.
M ice
N od
O ff.
P eacocks
Q uarrel.
R ats
S hriek.
T urtles
U nder
V ases.
W olves
X -raying
Y o-yoing
Z ebras.

Jamie Regan
Age: 9

ANIMALS

A
B unny
C an
D ance.
E lephants
F ight
G oats.
H ungry
I guanas
J ump
K razy.
L arge
M ice
N ibble
O ddly.
P andas
Q uietly
R egain
S trength.
T urtles
U ncovered
V aluable
W agons.
X -ray
Y ourself
Z ebra.

LaRae Patricia Goldsmith
Age: 8

DOGS AND POKER

Whoever thought of dogs playing poker?
Whoever it was, he must have been a joker.
Dogs can't tell the difference
  between deuces, aces, or one-eyed faces.
Imagine the day
  when dogs could play!

Rose Green
Age: 11

FROGS

The leap, they lop, they flip, they flop
Over logs frogs flip-flop
Over lily pads they slip and hop
Over the air catching flies
Flipping, flopping in the air
They leap, they lop, they flip, they flop

Johnny Luna
Age: 13

BEING THIRTEEN

Hard work builds character,
And that's what I've got.
I play the role of me,
And leave out what I'm not.

I've lived my life
To be all I can be,
But that's in my worktime,
Not in my free.

When can I slack off?
Where's my one day of freedom?
Oh, that's right, I don't get one,
I have a reputation.

Days and weeks go by,
Of my boring way of life.
I keeps going and never stops.
So I keep going, and boy do I strive.

Finally I stop to realize,
That I'm not one of a kind,
There are others,
With the same objective as mine.

So I keep my life the same,
Not easy to lead,
But I know about character.
So I will succeed!

I wonder if other people feel the way I do.

Amy Alletto
Age: 13

Nature is asleep
When the frostman is awake
Doing his cold job

Jordann Allen
Age: 9

I eat marrow,
Meat from the bones
I am a Homo habilis

Mara K. Whitehead

WINTER

Cold, windy, snowy
Christmas is in it
Snow is on the ground
It's my favorite season

John Daniel Tovado

Many falling leaves
Dancing with many colors
They catch my eyesight

Arielle Yoder

Hockey
aggressive, painful
shooting, crying, hurting
score a goal
Contact sport

Tyler White

I am Lucy
I eat bugs and nuts
And berries
I was found in a lake
And walked on two legs

Alexis E. McKenzie

THREE LITTLE DOGGIES

Once upon a time there were three doggies
And they all had something in common
Their names all started with the letter p
And they all had the same face and body
Blue eyes brown hair
So they were triplets

Audra Tromly

SCHOOL SOUNDS

Teachers educating kids.
Reach kids screeching.
Chairs clinging.
Footsteps thumping.
Doors squeaking.
Dogs barking.
Cars swishing snow.
Kids bellowing.
Music displaying its song.
Pencils working.

Kristin Van Sciver
Age: 8

BANANA BOY

Banana Boy is yellow
He is quite a funny fellow.
He has a smile on all the time
It makes me proud that he is mine.
Banana Boy is very cool
It's too bad I can't bring him to school.
He has a tropical appearance
Cool guy coming through, make a clearance.
No doubt Banana Boy is the coolest
Stuffed animal around!

Rachel Schittone
Age: 11

I am Homo sapiens
Sapiens
I dig for food
I look out for enemies
I look for shelter

Zachary Nelson

I am a scientist
I would find Homo erectus,
his bones
and we would find them
in the desert

Raleigh Jonscher

I am Homo habilis
I eat
I sleep
I eat marrow from bones

Fallon K. Osterberg

SYMPHONY

S imply great fun for
Y oung and old
M om's and dad's.
P erfectly amazing
H earing
O h so beautiful music.
N on-annoying music
Y elling in the end because it's great.

Kara Bausch
Age: 8

Deer
brown, white
fast, calm
runs through the bushes and leaves
hoofed mammals
Deer

Cary Shaffer
Age: 9

A STAR

Far, faraway
a star goes out to play
He rolls and runs
and has some fun
Until he yawns
for it is dawn.

Dyana Gutierrez
Age: 12

I'LL NEVER FORGET

I'll never forget the
lives that have perished.
I'll never forget the
burning buildings.
We'll never forget the
loved ones we have lost.
We shall never forget
the falling planes.
I'll never forget
the day of no good-byes.

Kendra Elder
Age: 12

THE WHITE SEASON

The white season is so cold.
It makes my hair prickle.
The hibernating animals are now asleep.
The migrating animals have already left.
We stay cozy in our homes and have warm soup.
'Til the green season comes back.

Zakaria Moumen
Age: 10

LOVE

Love is like a rope that is tied around two people.
Love is like a bond between a couple.
Love is like "I do"
When you're marrying someone.
Love is like a child that you bring into this world.
Love is like caring for someone that is in pain.
Love is something that is special
Between you and the person you love.

Xavier Farley ·
Age: 11

MOON

The moon up above,
oh look how it glows.
Men have looked upon it,
from under many a load.
And still to this day,
we on earth are looked upon,
by the beautiful face,
and then we sing a beautiful song.

Matthew Francis Fleming
Age: 12

A BABY KANGAROO

I know a baby kangaroo.
His mother nicknamed him Roo.
As he got bigger,
He played with Tigger.
He's in a show called Winnie the Pooh.

Elaine Gezahagne
Age: 14

IT'S HARD

It's hard to be somewhere
  when you're just not there.
It's hard to give it your all
  when your all's not there.
It's hard to put in your all
  when you can't give at all.
It's hard to keep your faith
  when all your faith seems to go.

Raul Quintana
Age: 13

SUMMER

Flowers blooming
Flowers shining in the sun
Water shimmering

Elizabeth Thal
Age: 11

THE TIDE

I went to the beach one day.
We walked to the bay.
I had so much fun in the tide,
  but a surfer hit me in the head.
It was a tie-dyed board.
I also got sucked in an undertow,
  so I guess it was a fun day.
Now I am tired,
  but it wasn't a boring day.

Patrick Kissell
Age: 11

Airplanes
smelly, loud
flying, soaring, diving
big, gas, fast, turn
slowing, stopping, going
shiny, leather
Car

Hayden Berge
Age: 10

Calm breeze
quiet, slow
starting, calming, quieting
silence, stillness, storm, nightmare
flowing, swirling, zigzagging
huge, horrible
Hurricane

Spencer Barringer

War is red
It sounds like muffled explosions
Far in the distance
It tastes of gunpowder
It smells like sulfur
And looks like a storm of lead and steel
It makes you feel alone

Brennan Gilbert
Age: 13